FACTS ABOUT 50 STATES

"ARE WE THERE YET, DAD?"

FLORIDA OR BUST

Rigby®

A Harcourt Achieve Imprint

www.Rigby.com
1-800-531-5015

ALABAMA

Nicknames:

**Yellowhammer State,
for the state bird;
Heart of Dixie, for its
location in the southern U.S.**

☞ Alabama was the first
state to build a monument
to an insect—the boll
weevil.

☞ People lived in
Russell Cave, in
Bridgeport, more than
9,000 years ago!

28 23
RANK IN SIZE / RANK IN POPULATION

SPEED
LIMIT
55

ALASKA

Nickname: The Great Frontier, because so much of Alaska is still unsettled

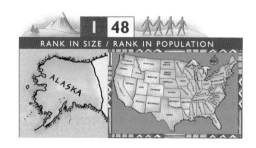

RANK IN SIZE / RANK IN POPULATION

☞ Alaska is so big that you could fit 487 Rhode Islands in it.

☞ Long days of sunshine—84 in a row—help Alaska's growing season and help produce record-size vegetables. One Alaskan cabbage reached 61 pounds!

ARIZONA

RANK IN SIZE / RANK IN POPULATION

Nicknames: Grand Canyon State, Copper State, Rattlesnake Heaven

☞ The Gila monster that lives in Arizona's deserts is the only poisonous lizard in the U.S.

☞ The oldest continuously inhabited city in America is Orabi, on the Hopi reservation.

ARKANSAS

27 33
RANK IN SIZE / RANK IN POPULATION

Nickname: **The Land of Opportunity,** **because of its many natural resources**

☞ Arkansas has the only diamond mine in North America. You can visit it and keep any diamonds you find.

☞ Hope is the state's watermelon capital—some melons have reached 195 pounds!

CALIFORNIA

Nickname: **Golden State,** **because of the gold rush of 1849**

3 1
RANK IN SIZE / RANK IN POPULATION

☞ California is home to General Sherman (a giant sequoia), the largest tree in the world. It weighs more than 6,167 tons—that's more than 740 elephants!

☞ The first talking cartoon was produced in 1928 by Walt Disney in Hollywood.

COLORADO

Nickname: Centennial State, because Colorado was granted statehood in 1876, exactly 100 years after the birth of our nation

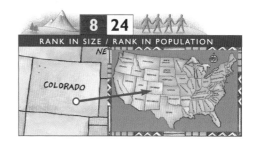

RANK IN SIZE / RANK IN POPULATION

8 24

COLORADO

☞ The largest silver nugget ever found in North America was discovered in Aspen in 1894—it weighed 1,840 pounds!

☞ Pike's Peak inspired Katharine Lee Bates to write "America the Beautiful" after a hiking trip.

CONNECTICUT

Nickname: **Constitution State, because the U.S. Constitution was based on Connecticut's rules for governing**

48 **29**
RANK IN SIZE / RANK IN POPULATION

☞ The football tackling dummy was invented at Yale University in 1889.

☞ *American Cookery*, by Amelia Simmons, is the first cookbook written by an American. It was published in Hartford in 1796.

DELAWARE

49 **45**
RANK IN SIZE / RANK IN POPULATION

Nickname: **The First State, because it was the first to approve the U.S. Constitution in 1787**

☞ The first beauty contest, Miss United States, was held in 1880. Thomas Edison was one of the judges.

☞ Log cabins were first introduced to North America in 1638 by Swedish immigrants who settled here.

FLORIDA

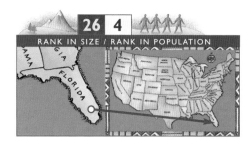

26 | 4
RANK IN SIZE / RANK IN POPULATION

Nicknames: **Sunshine State, Orange State, Alligator State**

☞ John Pennecamp Coral Reef State Park, near Key Largo, was the first undersea park in the continental U.S.

☞ Apollo 11, the first spacecraft to land men on the moon, was launched from Cape Canaveral on July 16, 1969.

GEORGIA

21 | 10
RANK IN SIZE / RANK IN POPULATION

Nicknames: **Peach State, Goober State, for peanuts**

☞ 1.5 billion pounds of peanuts are harvested every year in Georgia.

☞ The nation's first gold rush took place in Dahlonega in 1827.

☞ The Okefenokee is the nation's largest freshwater swamp.

HAWAII

Nickname: **Aloha State, because in its native language, *aloha* is said for hello and good-bye**

47	42
RANK IN SIZE	RANK IN POPULATION

☞ The Hawaiian alphabet has only 12 letters: a, e, h, i, k, l, m, n, o, p, u, and w.

☞ Barking Sands, on Kauai, is a beach that is sometimes quite dry, and when you walk on the sand, it makes a sound like a barking dog.

IDAHO

Nickname: **Gem State**

☞ Crystal Ice Cave has a frozen river, frozen waterfall, and other beautiful ice and stone formations.

☞ The Big Wood River has been called the "upside down river" because in one place it is about 100 feet deep and 4 feet wide, and nearby it is about 100 feet wide and 4 feet deep!

ILLINOIS

Nickname: **Land of Lincoln, because Abraham Lincoln lived here most of his life**

☞ The birthplace of atomic energy was the University of Chicago science lab, located under the school's athletic field.

☞ The first Ferris wheel was built in Illinois in 1893.

INDIANA

38 | 14
RANK IN SIZE / RANK IN POPULATION

Nickname: **Hoosier State, because a hasty greeting to newcomers was "Who's here?"**

☞ The Raggedy Ann doll was created in Indianapolis in 1914.

☞ Johnny Appleseed is buried in Indiana.

☞ The first long-distance auto race on a track took place on May 30, 1911 at the Indianapolis Motor Speedway.

IOWA

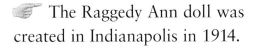

23 | 30
RANK IN SIZE / RANK IN POPULATION

Nicknames:

Hawkeye State, after the Sauk Chief, Black Hawk

☞ Iowa leads the nation in the percentage (99%) of people who can read and write.

☞ The Red Delicious apple was developed here.

☞ The shortest and steepest railroad in the U.S. is in Dubuque—the track is 296 feet long and 189 feet high!

KANSAS

KANSAS

OKLAHOMA

Nickname: **Sunflower State**

☞ Dorothy's House, the model house used in the filming of *The Wizard of Oz,* is in Liberal.

☞ Laura Ingalls Wilder wrote *Little House on the Prairie* based on her family's memories of Independence.

☞ "Big Brutus," a mining shovel weighing 11 million pounds, is now in a museum near West Mineral.

KENTUCKY

Nickname: **Bluegrass State**

RANK IN SIZE / RANK IN POPULATION
36 25

☞ Fort Knox guards the largest amount of gold in the world— more than $6 billion in gold bars.

☞ Cumberland Falls is the only place in the nation where moonbows form. On clear nights, the mist from the falls reflects the moon's light to make a colorful moonbow.

RANK IN SIZE / RANK IN POPULATION
33 22

LOUISIANA

Nickname: **Pelican State, for the large seabirds that populate its coast**

☞ In New Orleans, dead people are placed in above-ground tombs. The high water levels in the soil here would push coffins out of the ground!

☞ Jazz music originated in Louisiana.

MAINE

Nickname: **Pine Tree State, because of the state's tall pine forests**

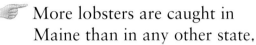

RANK IN SIZE / RANK IN POPULATION
39 40

☞ More lobsters are caught in Maine than in any other state.

☞ More than 60 lighthouses warn ships about Maine's rocky coastline.

☞ Maine makes more wooden toothpicks than any other state.

MARYLAND

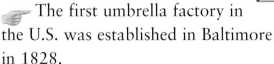

Nickname **Old Line State, to honor Maryland soldiers who "held" the line for General Washington in the Battle of Long Island in 1776**

RANK IN SIZE / RANK IN POPULATION
42 19

☞ The first umbrella factory in the U.S. was established in Baltimore in 1828.

☞ Francis Scott Key wrote "The Star-Spangled Banner" while watching the British attack Fort McHenry in 1814.

MASSACHUSETTS

RANK IN SIZE / RANK IN POPULATION 45 | 13

Nickname: **Bay State, because the entire eastern border opens into one bay or another**

☞ The first volleyball game was played in 1895 in Holyoke.

☞ *USS Constitution*, or "Old Ironsides," in Boston Harbor is the oldest warship in the world and is still a part of the U.S. Navy.

☞ Half of the nation's cranberries are grown in Massachusetts.

MICHIGAN

22 8
RANK IN SIZE / RANK IN POPULATION

Nickname: **Wolverine State, because of the early fur trade in wolverine pelts**

☞ No place in Michigan is more than 85 miles from a Great Lake.

☞ Battle Creek is called the "Cereal Bowl of America" because it produces more breakfast cereal than anywhere else.

☞ Henry Ford built his first workable automobile in Detroit in 1896.

MINNESOTA

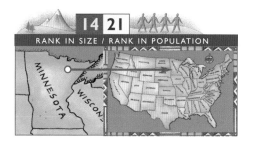

14 21
RANK IN SIZE / RANK IN POPULATION

Nickname: **North Star State, because of its far north location**

☞ The source of the Mississippi River is Lake Itasca.

☞ Cellophane transparent tape was invented in St. Paul in 1930.

☞ Statues of legendary lumberjack Paul Bunyan and Babe, his blue ox, are in Bemidji.

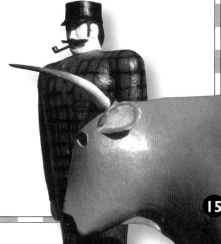

MISSISSIPPI

Nickname: **Magnolia State, for its many magnolia trees**

RANK IN SIZE / RANK IN POPULATION
31 31

☞ Petrified Forest, near Flora, contains giant stone trees dating back 30 million years.

☞ East Ship Island and West Ship Island were one island until 1969. In that year, Hurricane Camille cut the island in half.

MISSOURI

RANK IN SIZE / RANK IN POPULATION
18 17

Nickname:

Show Me State, because, according to folklore, the people of Missouri don't believe everything they hear—they want to be shown that something is true

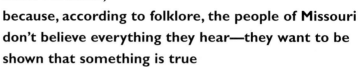

☞ Ice-cream cones and hot dogs were first seen in 1904 at the St. Louis World's Fair.

☞ The first parachute jump from an airplane was made in 1912.

MONTANA

RANK IN SIZE / RANK IN POPULATION
4 44

Nickname: **Treasure State, because of the gold and silver found in its mountains**

☞ Grasshopper Glacier is named for the swarms of grasshoppers that became trapped in its ice long ago and can still be seen today.

☞ More than 8,000 moose now live in Montana.

NEBRASKA

RANK IN SIZE / RANK IN POPULATION
15 38

Nickname: **Cornhusker State, because corn is Nebraska's leading crop and cornhusking contests are popular**

☞ J. Sterling Morton started Arbor Day in 1872—one million trees were planted.

☞ The only museum in the world dedicated to roller skating is near Lincoln.

☞ The largest mammoth fossil ever found was unearthed in 1922 near Wellfleet.

NEVADA

Nickname: **Silver State, because of its many silver mines**

☞ Nevada receives less rainfall than any other state.

☞ Hoover Dam was made with enough concrete to build a two-lane highway from New York to San Francisco.

☞ Mines in the Ruby Mountains produce the largest amount of the nation's gold.

NEW HAMPSHIRE

Nickname: **Granite State, for its large granite deposits**

RANK IN SIZE / RANK IN POPULATION
44 41

☞ The fastest wind ever recorded on Earth—231 miles per hour—was at the top of Mount Washington.

☞ Old Man of the Mountains is a natural formation on Profile Mountain that looks like the side of an old man's face.

NEW JERSEY

Nickname: **Garden State, for its many gardens**

RANK IN SIZE / RANK IN POPULATION
46 9

☞ In 1858, the nation's first dinosaur skeleton was found in Haddonfield. This dinosaur is known as Hadrosaurus.

☞ Samuel Morse demonstrated the first telegraph in 1838 in Morristown; Thomas Edison lit the first electric lamp in 1879 in Menlo Park.

NEW MEXICO

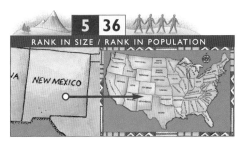

5 | 36
RANK IN SIZE / RANK IN POPULATION

Nickname: **Land of Enchantment, because of its scenic beauty and rich history**

☞ More chili peppers grow in the Rio Grande Valley than in any other place in the country.

☞ Smokey the Bear, a real bear cub, was rescued from a fire in Lincoln National Forest in 1950.

SMOKEY

NEW YORK

Nickname: Empire State, because when George Washington visited New York in 1783, he predicted it might become the center of a new empire

RANK IN SIZE / RANK IN POPULATION

30 | 3

☞ The first escalator was made in 1899.

☞ Under New York City lies 722 miles of subway track.

☞ Niagara Falls is one of the largest waterfalls in the world.

NORTH CAROLINA

Nickname: Tar Heel State, because tar was one of the state's earliest products

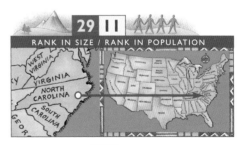

RANK IN SIZE / RANK IN POPULATION

29 | 11

☞ Roanoke Island was home to America's first English settlers in 1597.

☞ Cape Hatteras is called the "Graveyard of the Atlantic," because shifting sands caused many shipwrecks.

☞ The Wright brothers flew the first powered airplane at Kitty Hawk in 1903.

NORTH DAKOTA

Nickname: Peace Garden State, in honor of the International Peace Garden, which lies on the state's border with Manitoba, Canada

17 47
RANK IN SIZE / RANK IN POPULATION

NORTH DAKOTA

SOUTH

☞ The geographic center of North America is southwest of Rugby.

☞ Writing Rock, near Grenora, is a large boulder covered with Native American picture writing.

OHIO

Nickname: Buckeye State, because of its many buckeye trees

35 7
RANK IN SIZE / RANK IN POPULATION

OHIO

☞ Ohioans were the first to orbit Earth (John Glenn, 1962) and to step on the moon (Neil Armstrong, 1969).

☞ Ohio's chickens produce the largest number of eggs—about 7 million a year.

☞ Cincinnati has the first zoo in the U.S. dedicated to insects.

OKLAHOMA

Nickname: Sooner State, because some settlers were there "sooner," or before, the government opened the land for settlement

19 27

RANK IN SIZE / RANK IN POPULATION

☞ About 50,000 new settlers rushed in to claim land on April 22, 1889.

☞ Oil, or "black gold," was discovered in Oklahoma in 1928. There are even oil wells on the front lawn of the state capitol!

OREGON

Nickname: **Beaver State**

☞ The world's smallest official park, originally created for snail races, is 24 inches across and is on a traffic island in Portland.

☞ The world's shortest river is the D River—it's 58 feet long.

☞ Sea Lion Cave, near Florence, is the world's largest sea cave and is home to many sea lions.

wow!

PENNSYLVANIA

Nickname: **Keystone State, because it was the center, or the keystone, of the original 13 states**

RANK IN SIZE / RANK IN POPULATION
32 6

☞ Philadelphia had the nation's first zoo in 1874.

☞ Pittsburgh had the world's first radio station (KDKA) in 1920.

☞ The world's largest chocolate factory is in southeastern Pennsylvania.

RHODE ISLAND

Nickname: **Little Rhody, because it's the smallest state**

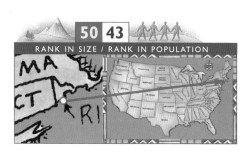

RANK IN SIZE / RANK IN POPULATION
50 43

☞ The Rhode Island Red is the chicken that made poultry raising a major industry in the U.S.

☞ This state is made up of 36 islands.

☞ The oldest schoolhouse in the nation stands in Portsmouth. It was built in 1716.

SOUTH CAROLINA

Nickname: **Palmetto State, for its graceful palmetto trees**

40 | 26
RANK IN SIZE / RANK IN POPULATION

☞ The first shots of the Civil War were fired at Fort Sumter.

☞ The nation's only true stork, the wood stork, is an endangered species here.

☞ The world's largest collection of stock cars is in a museum at a raceway in Darlington.

SOUTH DAKOTA

16 | 46
RANK IN SIZE / RANK IN POPULATION

Nickname:
Mount Rushmore State

☞ The Badlands is an area of spectacular natural beauty that was created by erosion.

☞ When the Crazy Horse Memorial is completed, it will be the world's largest sculpture. Crazy Horse's head is about 88 feet tall. His arm is 263 feet long!

TENNESSEE

Nickname: **Volunteer State, because Tennesseans were among the first to volunteer for wars**

34 | 16
RANK IN SIZE / RANK IN POPULATION

☞ More people visit the Great Smoky Mountains National Park than any other national park.

☞ The first guide dog for the blind in the U.S. was Buddy, a German shepherd that lived in Nashville.

☞ No place in the world records more music than Nashville.

TEXAS

Nickname: Lone Star State, because of the single star on its flag

RANK IN SIZE / RANK IN POPULATION
2 2

☞ In 1836, many people died at the Alamo, fighting for independence from Mexico.

☞ No state produces more oil or cotton. No state raises more beef.

☞ An average of 125 tornadoes blow through the state each year—more than any other state.

UTAH

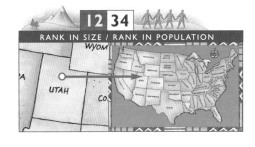

RANK IN SIZE / RANK IN POPULATION
12 34

Nickname: Beehive State, because the people are as busy as bees

☞ Thousands of dinosaur bones have been discovered in Dinosaur National Monument.

☞ The Great Salt Lake has a higher salt content than any ocean.

☞ Seagulls have a monument in Salt Lake City because they saved crops from an invasion of crickets in 1848.

VERMONT

Nickname: **Green Mountain State, because of its tree-covered mountains**

43 49
RANK IN SIZE / RANK IN POPULATION

☞ Montpelier is the nation's largest producer of maple syrup.

☞ Concord Academy, established in 1823, was the first school dedicated to the training of teachers.

VIRGINIA

RANK IN SIZE / RANK IN POPULATION 37 | 12

Nickname: **Mother of Presidents, because eight U.S. presidents were born here**

☞ Jamestown was the first permanent English settlement in America in 1607.

☞ The Revolutionary War's last battle was fought at Yorktown in 1781. Eleven major battles of the Civil War were fought in Virginia. The surrenders that ended both these wars also took place in Virginia.

WASHINGTON

Nickname: **Evergreen State, because of its many evergreen trees**

RANK IN SIZE / RANK IN POPULATION 20 | 15

☞ The most snow to fall in one year in North America occurred at Rainier Paradise Ranger Station—a total of 1,122 inches.

☞ An airplane factory in Everet is the largest building in the U.S. covers 47 acres.

WEST VIRGINIA

Nickname: **Mountain State, because of its rugged, hilly landscape**

☞ The New River Gorge Bridge is the world's longest steel-arch bridge. It is 1,700 feet long.

☞ The town of Romney changed hands between Union and Confederate soldiers 56 times during the Civil War.

☞ The first tree with Golden Delicious apples was discovered in 1775.

WISCONSIN

Nickname: Badger State, because in the 1920s, miners lived in caves they dug out of hillsides, like badgers burrowing underground

25 | 18
RANK IN SIZE / RANK IN POPULATION

☞ Wisconsin produces more milk than any other state—enough to fill 11 Olympic-sized pools a day!

☞ The world's biggest chunk of cheese weighed 345,000 pounds, or the weight of 43 elephants.

WYOMING

Nickname: Equality State, because Wyoming women were the first women in the U.S. to vote

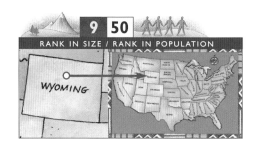

9 | 50
RANK IN SIZE / RANK IN POPULATION

☞ In 1872, Yellowstone became the nation's first national park.

☞ At least twice as many cows as people live in the state.

☞ One ton of coal per second is dug at Black Thunder, the largest coal mine in America.